PARADISO DIASPORA

Poetry and Fiction

Ing Grish (with artwork by Thomas Nozkowski)
Borrowed Love Poems
My Heart Is That Eternal Rose Tattoo
My Symptoms
I Was a Poet in the House of Frankenstein
Forbidden Entries
Lowell Connector (with Clark Coolidge, Michael Gizzi,
    Bill Barrette, and Celia Coolidge)
Big City Primer (with Bill Barrette)
Hawaiian Cowboys
Berlin Diptychon (with Bill Barrette)
Edificio Sayonara
Radiant Silhouette: New and Selected Work, 1974–1988
Corpse and Mirror
Broken Off by the Music
The Sleepless Night of Eugene Delacroix
Sometimes
The Reading of an Ever-Changing Tale
Crossing Canal Street

Artist's Books

Andalusia (with Leiko Ikemura)
Movies as a Form of Reincarnation (with Archie Rand)
100 More Jokes from The Book of The Dead (with Archie Rand)
Double Headed Creature Feature (with Max Gimblett
    and Tobin Hines)
New York Islands (with Martin Noel)
Letter from Marina (with Bodo Korsig)
Architecture of Ink (with Dan Walsh)
Genghis Chan: Private Eye (with Ed Paschke)
Dream Hospital (with Robert Therrien)
Picadilly or Paradise (with Trevor Winkfield)
Postcards from Trakl (with Bill Jensen)
Giant Wall (with Jürgen Partenheimer)
Dragon's Blood (with Toni Grand)

Monographs and Criticism

The Passionate Spectator: Essays on Art and Poetry
David Reed: Leave Yourself Behind
Fred Tomaselli: Monsters of Paradise
Max Gimblett (with Wystan Curnow)
Randy Hayes: The World Reveiled
Dazzling Water, Dazzling Light (with Pat Steir and Barbara Weidle)
James Castle: The Common Place
Suzan Frecon
Original Sin: The Visionary Art of Joe Coleman
   (with Jim Jarmusch and Harold Schechter)
Mary Heilmann: Farbe und Lust / Color and Passion
The United States of Jasper Johns
Ed Moses: A Retrospective of the Paintings and Drawings, 1951–1996
In the Realm of Appearances: The Art of Andy Warhol
A.R. Penck

Editor

Fairfield Porter: The Collected Poems, with Selected Drawings (with David Kermani)

PARADISO DIASPORA

John Yau

 PENGUIN POETS

PENGUIN BOOKS

Published by the Penguin Group
Penguin Group (USA) Inc., 375 Hudson Street, New York, New York 10014, U.S.A.
Penguin Group (Canada), 90 Eglinton Avenue East, Suite 700, Toronto, Ontario, Canada M4P 2Y3
(a division of Pearson Penguin Canada Inc.)
Penguin Books Ltd, 80 Strand, London WC2R 0RL, England
Penguin Ireland, 25 St Stephen's Green, Dublin 2, Ireland (a division of Penguin Books Ltd)
Penguin Group (Australia), 250 Camberwell Road, Camberwell, Victoria 3124, Australia
(a division of Pearson Australia Group Pty Ltd)
Penguin Books India Pvt Ltd, 11 Community Centre, Panchsheel Park, New Delhi-110 017, India
Penguin Group (NZ), cnr Airborne and Rosedale Roads, Albany, Auckland 1310, New Zealand
(a division of Pearson New Zealand Ltd)
Penguin Books (South Africa) (Pty) Ltd, 24 Sturdee Avenue, Rosebank, Johannesburg 2196, South Africa

Penguin Books Ltd, Registered Offices:
80 Strand, London WC2R 0RL, England

First published in Penguin Books 2006

10 9 8 7 6 5 4 3 2 1

Page xi constitutes an extension of this copyright page.

LIBRARY OF CONGRESS CATALOGING IN PUBLICATION DATA
Yau, John, 1950–
Paradiso diaspora / John Yau.
p. cm.
ISBN 0 14 30.3715 3
I. Title.
PS3575.A9P37 2006
811'.54—dc22 2005056723

Printed in the United States of America
Set in Bembo
Designed by Ginger Legato

For Eve and Cerise

For my sins I live in the city of New York

—Ted Berrigan

Acknowledgments

Author's note: I would like to thank the following magazines, and their editors, for their hospitality and care: *American Poetry Review, Bat City Review, Conjunctions, Crowd, Interim, 1913: un journal des formes, The Saint Ann's Review,* and *Verse.*

"After" was published as a broadside by Dolphin Press (Maryland Institute College of Art). "Broken Sonnet" was published as a broadside by Center for the Book Arts, New York. "A Sheaf of Pleasant Voices" was chosen by Robert Creeley to appear in *The Best American Poetry 2002* (New York: Scribner Poetry, 2002). "Ghost Guest" first appeared in *Mark di Suvero: Indoors* (New York: Knoedler & Company, 2005). "The Morning after That One" was included in *110 Stories: New York Writes After September 11,* edited by Ulrich Baer (New York: New York University Press, 2002). "Andalusia," with artwork by Leiko Ikemura, was published in a limited edition by Weidle Verlag (Bonn) and Black Square Editions (New York) in 2006.

Contents

V

VI

PARADISO DIASPORA

Introduction

It had to be from someone whose grandparents were born in Shanghai
not the city's greatest citizens, but certainly among the sober ones
to make their small now eroded mark
It had to be from a distant or dissolute descendant (yes, *moi*)
who can sing praises unworthy of even a flicker of your attention

Doesn't this sound like it might turn into a love poem or a prayer
Well, you are wrong, because a man of the people,
which I am not nor will I ever be,
doesn't single out one above all others
as this is a hierarchical construction
and therefore undemocratic and antihumanist

It had to be from someone whose virtues do not include stubbornness,
patience, gentleness, loyalty, or truthfulness

It had to be from someone who could take my place
after I left the room
never to return

It had to be from someone who didn't exist
before this poem
began writing itself down

I.

Andalusia (1)

Time quietly peers in each window
but only the children find it funny

The second necklace we wear is the horizon
circling our waists and throats as the flowers
splash the sky with twilight and constellations
map out the mishaps settling above the city

Abracadabras and horoscopes are impatient
with sleep and calligraphy

Grant me a sheet of paper that will not turn to ash
and this hand will write down afternoon's clouds
while you are hidden in my eyes, it is enough
this sheet of paper where I have hidden you
in these days of smoke and candle flames

Grant me time to pause and inquire of the clouds
if they have concealed you in their tears
behind a red sky in which the moon briefly flies

Grant me a sheet of paper that we might
live near the heat we once made when our hands
pelted the sky with ink and paint

Margins of thought curled like eyelashes
ask them if they remember us now
that our names are forgotten

Andalusia (2)

Rooftop roosters announce a new regime
Even at night, guided by the moon,

the sky can never find a cloud that fits
but, for the painter, each cloud is snug

Still, it is the sheet of paper that I want
and the inks that can keep these lovers safe

in the small garden where even the birds
have stopped to look at their reflections

Andalusia (3)

Are not clouds sketches for a sculpture
that will never emerge from stone

The neck of a cat visits you at night
Are the stars still spies loyal to no one

All that is left are these jackals
wandering across a glittering field

Our shadows have floated into the sky
leaving our other shadows behind

No need to inquire where or how
Someday you too may need this garden

Andalusia (4)

Was it a madman who claimed
there is no reason to remember these stones

descending from an oscillating sky
Are you here to pick clean these emerald, amethyst,

pearl and topaz leaves and branches
By the gold border white jasmine shed their petals

and the carnelian's red shadow awaits a mortar and pestle
A thousand miles of clouds to climb the tower

We will leave no footprints in the dust
nor ever again touch the swaying grass

Not even particles of our names
will be sifted from this storm of lines

Andalusia (5)
(Postcards)

Mother-of-pearl-cloud
clads clump and clod

Quillons and spandrels
Curlicues and spikes

Irregular medallion
Lustrous heron

Emerald tears sparkle
in sky's mortar and pestle

Andalusia (6)

Above against below beside near and around
Outside buttressed by imaginary flowers
Within a storm of letters echoing arches
Beneath a serpentine cloud dipped in ink
Near a circle of lilies, each steeped petal
Beside twin strands of hexagonal tears
Above a shadow tracing its shadows

Andalusia (7)

Story of flanking rosettes, palmettes, and petals

Story of alloys and allies, metal mouthpieces and fleshy mouths

Story of caparisoned elephants imprisoned in silk

Story of sky's pillared pavilion
and a dress unraveled by butterflies

Story of apricot, lilac, pistachio, and blue cobalt

Story of flowers that do not grow on earth
and must be turned in the light to be seen

Story about beginning before a story begins,
and becomes a story about beginning

Andalusia (8)

I offer no proof that we were here
in sky's tent beneath stars' arrows

Written in invisible ink on smoke
rising above the night we were together

I offer no proof that we were ever here
folded together in a cloud's folds

now that it is an exquisite picture
that anyone can visit

In the Lion Night

1.

Where will we go and fret
clouds' reproaches be met

our sighs be sent
our sentences kept

our tears returned
and all our kisses mended

2.

Tonight, I want your kisses
gathering on my mouth
I cannot escape this thought
nor do I want to, even though
you have traveled to a foreign city
                        with another man.

Poems for Leiko (1)

Today the sun is a cloud
sprouting green hair

A waterlogged mast
rises from mist

They meet in a room
best described as anonymous

In a darkened room
a different room

pierced by a beam of light
scrutinizing reflections

rows of empty faces
not looking back

they believe the words
birds form in the sky

possess human faces
Is that who is peering down

from crenellated clouds
Is that who is just now

stepping out of the clock to sing
Today a blue flower ascends

through layers of a fiery lake
Today they meet in a room

best described as synonymous
These are pictures of things

they do not see on the wall
before them

ghostly songs haunting the stories
they try again and again to tell

Poems for Leiko (2)
First Interlude

It is red when the gray
starts swelling around

the base of the sky's stalk
and the threat

or thread of the future
no longer seems quite so far away

Could we not one day
meet on the other side of the mirror

from where the dust gathers
Could we not stay

in that room of
difficult light

Poems for Leiko (3)

Second Interlude

This pitted figurine
is a monument

to the perfection of torsos
seized from spheres of smoke

Am I not a slave
to your obedience

when my hands
describe you in the dark

Poems for Leiko (4)

I am here
I am not here

Can these places
not be the same place

a voice calls to the birds
interred in the mirroring sky

II.

Conversation after Midnight

The civilization of green ants
met last week or month
(your sense of time a concept
I don't yet understand
and besides I wasn't there)
and they elected me to come here,
even though me was still not me or even an I,
an unarticulated murmur maybe that,
at best some dust of unlikely possibility,
I was nevertheless elected to be
among you, to arrive and to periodically whimper
howl stir scream cry
in a black spring night
gone sour with images of the moon
(O oarless alabaster boat)
(O pearly O sitting high above the savannah)
so many poets still call on,
as if it's the next-door neighbor,
a ubiquitous presence signifying
the right proportion of magic and tragedy
when they want to let everyone know
how divine they have become in the interim
kissed by capital G you might say
but I need not tell you that you are hardly divine
a lump is more like it if it is what you are
my name is Cerise Tzara Aschheim Yau
I am your daughter
I have been here a little over a month
crying shitting eating sleepless restless
as I extend my arms and kick my feet
and I can see that you are perplexed by what
I am trying to tell you through the infant
you hold in your hands, the one you
think of as your daughter
which she is, but I too am your daughter,

I who am an I, you, me, two three,
the one elected by the green ants
Their leader whispered something
(was I to repeat it word for word
as if such repetition is accurate
a higher form of mimesis than trompe l'oeil)
something I have forgotten during
the during and enduring from the to the,
here and there not yet having hardwired
their coordinates within the celestial tumult
something in words about and through them perhaps
I can't remember which is why no amount of
beseeching is going to yield anything more from me
than I am the poem yes I am the one
you want to write or be written by
you boob or should I say *Boobus Santicmonius*
I am the poem
you need to write to and for
the one that isn't the one
but one of the ones who might
step out from the flickering skyline of transparent shadows
and say to you years from now
hey old farting sag face
dim bulb in a dark and gloomy night
why did you spend years
shitting all that goop onto pristine white page
after white page
And you will smile
knowing I know the answer
knew it before here became
the time-space continuum
I inhabit
but this is a conversation that will unfold
at and in another time right now being
right now I am hungry
so go
get me something warm to drink
will you Bud

And hey mister whoever you are
you better quit
calling me
Pipalotti Poopsalot
Starvin' Marvin
Crusty Punkin and Kid
I gotta name
Why doncha use it

First Song after Cerise

Soon I will be a purple centaur with blue hair
Watching ink tumble beside phosphorescent stars
Go stuff the rest of your head in an attic
                          where it is cold and sparse
Will you don these moon goggles and find the bear
Who got lost behind the lady's chocolate covered cars
I live in an alcove of mermaids but do not know what to wear
Who is pointing to the mountaintop I found on Mars
Enamel moon, farinaceous wisps. Why not stare?
In this atmosphere the painter dwells in stolen air
Now that you are no longer a vicar
Twirling the ghost of his chewed cigar
I will tell you what it means to undergo extensive repair
And how I briefly became a blue centaur with purple hair

Second Song after Cerise

If I am wearing purple pants
Then the Empire State can be purple too

Listen to me before you turn off the light
Tempest Fusion means "time cries," right

Third Song after Cerise

Written for
and on a flute

turned from
music's lathe

its blue soot
parting clouds

to soap
and bathe

III.

After

I slum among crumbs, a spotted shadow
Before I become a surrogate republic
For you, O decorated cyborg
O Comrade Snowflake in a lonely pool

Before I become a surrogate republic
I blushed fossils with phosphorus
O Comrade Snowflake in a lonely pool
I still sing faithfully to each and every vertebra

I blushed fossils with phosphorus
Is this really your final answer
I still sing faithfully to each and every vertebra
I kiss each mouth you offer

Is this really your final answer
For you, O decorated cyborg
I kiss each mouth you offer
I slum among crumbs, a spotted shadow

Robert Desnos Writes

What strange sound glided the length of the bannister down to where the
transparent apple was dreaming?

I don't know the answer to that question or the one before, or the ones
before that. A key chain without keys is all that I feel beneath my pillow.
Now how will I ever find my way back to the Saskatchewan night car?

I nudge him again, but he has already fallen asleep at the table. And, as if his
head has been removed by one-armed bandits and placed in a copper basket
lined with potted plants, he has started speaking into the waterlogged tape
recorder:
If your horoscope mentions scissors, scorpions, or scrapbooks, you should
post an ad for a woman who can prove to you her name is Robert Desnos.
She will look like me and she will sound like me, but the poetry she writes
will be neither hers nor mine.

Please copy what I have said, including the part that begins, "Please
copy . . ."

Shortly after the last clock in town tolls midnight, black carriages begin
lining up outside The New Archive Luncheonette. A swarm of iridescent
gnats hovers above the main shed of the obsolete gondola repair depot. In an
adjacent frame, two policemen discuss ways to improve their uniforms, how
their epaulets might be emphasized to greater effect. On a quaint suburban
street near the fireworks factory, a team of champion wrestlers practices
hauling the corpse of a pink walrus into an illegally parked armored car.

This is how we meet, beneath a billboard of a burning city, above a car
named after a beach, in a room ablaze with citron stripes. You are painting,
and the room is filled with a warm liquid called "light." Don't bash the
squash, you scribble in the air with your brush. The sky is a black horse
pawing the ocean, I scribble back with my fingers. Both of you are brazen
with gibberish, the smoke scribbles in its entrails.

The fortune teller looks up from her deck of cards. Why don't you see yourself as a mathematical object, a creeping blue buttercup, one inkling plum among many? I do, which is why I want to report how I found the world, the poet whispers to the philosopher who has accompanied him to this infernal basement.

Where did you say you were taking me?

But you are smoke, and I and my many unembraced selves cannot carry you anywhere, because you go wherever you want. O smoke, want is never the issue on which your laws are written.

Yes, the smoke heard itself answering, though it was sure it wasn't doing the speaking.

Yes, I am poetry and its residue settling onto the wig of a man who appears to have fallen asleep, all alone beneath his tiny wooden star.

Ghost Guest
For Mark di Suvero

At dawn crows
gather around
heaven's stove

waiting for Hermes
to crumple
a purple shawl

into a pavilion
of clouds
gathering beneath a bridge

This is where ripe plums
can fill a plaza
with perfume

where, in the garden,
a bear dips his nose
in blackberry ink

and writes a poem
Smoke rises from
cottages clustered

around the pagoda
A butterfly drops down
and admits it loves

shadows sweeping past
Lantern light pauses
in the corner of a cold studio

Tuz

In the village of mummies
there are no letters

to the future
The rest is nearly wrapped

Similar shadows
coexist beside the lake

It began with the feeling
one gets from eating lemons

This winter is
not like any other

Every morning just before the sun
climbs its ladder

another child is found
dead in the park

leaning against
the statue of Vladimir

his serrated neck
a secret hiding place

It is too late to start again
amid cathodes, motorcades, and noodles

First the voice
then the face decays

Monogram Studios I

After a solid income-earner recounts his dream
to a phony magician he meets on a three-star bus

he steals a gun in a desperate attempt to distract himself
from suspecting that his new wife is secretly

the eldest daughter of a retired Roman general
who is suspected of driving his first two wives insane

Before a woman decides to hire a blind carpenter
to bury her husband behind the patio

overlooking a hospital for recovering counterfeiters
she decides to impersonate a distraught nurse

by climbing onto the windswept, bird-infested
ledge of a condemned skyscraper

When a novelist's tarnished assistant
is seduced by a handsome patsy

recovering from an unfortunate lapse
that occurred during hypnosis

a stylishly dressed thief convinces herself
that she has inadvertently learned

what the members of a crime
magazine coven have up their sleeves

Mistaking the huge green star mounted
on the prison tower for a sign

the three newly arrived visitors
from outer space decide that it would be best

if they make bronze impressions of their footprints
and mail them to their Hittite counterparts

The retired neophyte explains that the fabulous
will become much less nebulous after the yearly

drought passes, but a few miles away
on the same paved road, there are many

splendid views of goatskin tents,
plastic surgeons, and dried meat

Set in the massive lobby of
a burning public building

which the audience realizes
is an inaccurate rendition,

four mice in bowlers and tuxedos
devise an elaborate hoax

which requires that one of them is reincarnated
while the others stare on in disbelief

Monogram Studios II

Roped centaurs and their seashore chaperones
snore in the dumpster behind the motel

A gabber in gabardine thaws in the garage
In the kitchen, polishing silverware,

especially the ceremonial forks
their extravagantly elongated tines,

the chauffeur, scruffy boots,
shabby uniform and stained collar

his unmistakable silhouette
worming its way across the ceiling

Among the sprockets turning slowly
beneath the infamous Victorian calendar,

its carefully rendered drawings of nail parings,
the audience immediately recognizes that,

while relatively likeable, a rebellious
but not necessarily youthful lycanthrope

repeatedly forgets to apply cosmetics
to the latest stool pigeon to defect

from the catacombs running beneath
the hospice, gas station, and caravanserai,

before happily defecating in
his richly ornamented mail pouch

One spawned, the other spurned,
and between these two fortresses

the farmers tilted their cold brows
toward the ashen sun

Enduring another humdrum shift
until he is unexpectedly inspired

to deliver a necklace of crushed black orchids
to the suspicious wife of a superstitious embalmer,

but his best friend, who moonlights
as a rickshaw repairman, is mistaken

for a well-preserved denizen of Pompeii,
and accidentally released,

like a jar of flesh-colored dust,
into the path of an oncoming marchioness

Once the implant has been inserted
into a part of the brain the host

seldom visits, the operating team
opens the hall window

and vanishes into the warm suburban air
Curlicues of smoke appear in the mirror

Evening arrives
in bright red bunches

Coming Attractions

1.

Not only is the first shot of half-clothed women,
their eyes averted as they scamper past an ogre

roasting marshmallows in the groove of a dried-up riverbed,
but, in an adjacent aisle of this outdoor market,

rosy-cheeked children have started weeping within
earshot of their inexplicably demented parents

Palm trees sway outside an impoverished train station
A rusty axe climbs above the mist-enshrouded horizon

2.

Not only does the amnesiac detective forget who has been murdered,
but the murderer, unbeknownst to him, wants to marry his ex-ex,

before transporting him to a small two-car garage
where he can agonize over why he shouldn't pretend

to be a wildly successful industrialist
suffering from an incurable malady

3.

Not only does a thrice-resurrected actor
imbibe a secret so horrible that everyone

suddenly stops fidgeting with their gadgets,
but smoke rises in spurts from the orchestra pit

and the earth beneath our feet
begins yawning with alarming regularity

4.

Not only does a group of sales clerks gathered
in the lobby of a tropical potboiler discover

they are no longer witty and seductive,
but rivulets of melting rouge run down the flowered walls

like carriages on their way to a picnic
overlooking an upgraded battlefield

5.

Not only does a wealthy matron's adventures culminate
in an illicit affair with a genuine clairvoyant

who has awoken from a deep sleep brought on
by poorly mixed aphrodisiacs, but the mournful dirges

spinning in that leaky jukebox you call your head
lead to a herd of blue elephants towing a barge across ice

Doll Lullaby

The herds are groomed and the flock
is starting to burn right on schedule,
its flames licking the clocks
that keep an eye on all our dabbling in paradise.
Now that I have finished my loathsome tasks,
as well as counted caterpillars, clowns, and canaries,
I will stop being an urchin and the archer's favorite toad.
I will retreat to the garage and count my toes,
always a pleasant Pythagorean reminder
that I am marble and pillow.
Time does not shade my face,
but I am prone to dents and eclipses of the eyelid
that send forth tears in search of fictitious mirrors.
In my social circle, tenderness is parceled out like bad cake
cemented by frosting's cheerless colors.
Did you hear them talking in the other room?
the one who recounted her years of roaming the aisles,
and the one whose marrow turned to fog and ice.
This is only the beginning. Outside, the clouds are lower
than they were yesterday, pressed down by equestrian sky.
Listen, Black Star, I followed your instructions
until the kangaroos bounded back to their cave.
I kissed a pink crustacean and witnessed
an unofficial decapitation
and did not open my hands or heart.
I confessed that I was born in a hut
overlooking a harbor straddled with scum,
a store whose shelves are lined with oily cardboard,
a high rise inhabited by insidious fireflies.
I was released near an outlet mall, a prison, and banquet hall.
Adolescent monkeys leapt over my first reminiscences
while their hairless elders masticated my older siblings.
I am the disowned descendant of a spinning wheel.
I have a name, but I will no longer abuse it.

Still-Life

Bread hardens
into stone

A wolf bleeds
in a doorway

I have burned
down the sky

Trees stop
listening

Birds put away
their pens

As always,
the moon

is sterile
and perpendicular

Mouth filled
with snow

rain and mud
How many times

will I die
before it is over

There are not enough
fingers in a day

Your Cyborg
(after André Breton)

Your cyborg with the hairline of a woodchuck fireman
at the threshold of heaven's likeness
with the houseguest's walkie-talkie
with an outcast's walkie-talkie
in the telekinesis of a tightwad
Your cyborg with a coconut lisp
and a laudable maharishi's bunion steeple
with the telekinesis of whopping microbes on whooping echoes
with the tonsillectomy of ruffled ambrosia and glee
Your cyborg with the tonsillectomy of a stamped hotshot
with the tonsillectomy of a dolphin that opposes and clutches its eyepiece
with the tonsillectomy of an unblushing stool pigeon
Your cyborg with strontium eyesight
inserted behind a chime's wrongdoing
with bruises of editions pawned from a houseboat's neuralgia
Your cyborg with the bruises of sledgehammers
pilfered from a housefly's room
and of steel on panic
Your cyborg with showcases of eucalyptus chandeliers
and a foxhole with dominoes beneath icicles
Your cyborg with write-offs of mathematics
Your cyborg with finials of lullabies and acidity of the hearth
with finials of multiplied hazards
Your cyborg with arrivals of martyrs, beehives, and midwifery
of probation and an angleworm's neuralgia
with arrows of sealskin and roadrunner
and the misspelling of *whelk* and *millampere*
Your cyborg with legerdemain of flashlights
with muckrakers of cloisters and despots
Your cyborg with calisthenics of electrocardiogram pizzazz
Your cyborg with ink's forbearing
with ringworm forbearing
and junior varsity spittoons dropping
Your cyborg with barometer necromancy
Your cyborg with a throwaway vampire of gold

with tubing in the very bedposts of tortoni
with nighthawk breastplates
Your cyborg with breastplates of marriageable moments
Your cyborg with breastplates of the Ruffian Crusade
with breastplates of the rogue's speedometer beneath diabolical diagrams
Your cyborg with the belvedere of an unforgiving fantasia
with the belvedere of a glabrous clearing
Your cyborg with a backswept biscuit flirting vestigially
with a backswept quintet
with a backswept lightweight
with a narcosis of rubbed stoops and whimsical chameleons
with the dross of a glen where ooze has been drooping
Your cyborg with the histamine of a chanteuse and an arthropod
with whopping shale plutocrats and their insincere penises
Your cyborg with buzzards of a sanitarium and an ashtray
Your cyborg with swatch buzzards
Your cyborg with sprite buzzards in an isosceles shack
Your cyborg with the shack of a mink and a playboy
Your cyborg with a shack of secretion and angry switchboards
Your cyborg with a shack of miscegenation
Your cyborg with eyepieces full of tea time and technetium
with eyepieces of purple pantheism and majestic negligence
Your cyborg with eyepieces of Waterloo to be drowned in privacy
Your cyborg with eyepieces of woodchuck under the azalea
Your cyborg with eyepieces of waterworks
of lexicons of alley easel firebug

A Sheaf of Pleasant Voices

There are rooftops
made of cloud remnants

gathered by a trader
dabbling in car parts and burlap

At night, I dive onto the breeze
fermenting above the dirt

and dream that I am a crocodile
a tin of shoe polish, an audience of two

In the morning, before the smallest yawn
becomes a noodle, I am offered

a ribbon of yellow smoke
I opt for fuzzy rocks and clawed water

and, of course, the perishable window
I am one of the last computer

chain errors to be illuminated
I tell you there are rooftops

on which the moon stops
being a cold jewel

And one by one the mountains
begin their descent from

the chambers of a lost book

Before Tears End

All that windshield steam no wonder
you needed the minute you got up
stumbled onto next perfumed ice
collecting sinking floorboard anchors
Hey did you hear about the politician
who came and stayed until he was never
seen again though his voice was recorded
for posterity which is now a professional
descendant on a horse arouses tree-house
ruckus among miners busy rubbing nuggets
concocting who might answer their twin
memorial tower of store-bought prayers
meticulously realistic loon in hula skirt
holding fresh poppies from Mantova
a talking apple tree infected by slugs
Might not this lanky diamond chiaroscuro
symptom patrol know difference
between upper reception
and lower erection decide
neither headband good enough
to wipe clean hexagonal animal dust
scrawled in mechanical slump
Might not furniture include part of future
excavated and arranged in old people's trash
Might not this destination be the carnival
you managed to void the morning
you set out in your pumps and pantaloons

Carfax Abbey

Sky convulses into a great fart
a bubble of pleasantness

floating toward the *Kether*
I didn't know being American

meant that I could get a job
parking jalopies underground

near where *Hades*
in the Shade

that swollen
destination

welcomes shoppers,
slurrers, and loppers

accompanying that
arduous chassis ballad

that pallid hammer belly
while children steal curls

in a meadow
of human orifices

that I could write
filthy elegies

in my sleep
on weekends

under tricycles
near televisions

broadcasting beavers and badgers
revealing their lesser aspects

that hamlets emit
sky-colored flames

a sure sign of industriousness
fanning wings of inertia

Did you enjoy your oval
auxiliary skeletons

mementos of an unpleasant incursion
pinup ambassador gang

Did you learn to cease
investing commotion

lest you become ghost
to hooligans of uncertain origin

New moon brings
no new memo

Pond rusts
in puerile bliss

Headless dancers display
irritated enigmas

flickering with
guzzled reciprocity

Would you like
to exchange your wig

for an alternative grammar
smooth and silky

like underwear
posted beyond

your jurisdiction
Has everyone

brought his or her
footstool and ammunition

Is a visitation, vexation, or hex
parking noises in your remote

control communications center
Honestly, I didn't know

being American
meant

that you could
shit in the driver's seat

Broken Sonnet

The world weeps. There are no tears
To be found. It is deemed a miracle.
The president appears on screens
In villages and towns, in cities in jungles
And jungles still affectionately called cities.
He appears on screens and reads a story.
Whose story is he reading and why?
What lessons are to be learned from this story
About a time that has not arrived, will not arrive, is here?
Time of fire and images of fire climbing toward the sun
Time of precious and semi-precious liquids
Time of a man and a woman doused in ink
Rolling across streams and down valleys
Trying to leave some string of words behind.

Life in the Leafy Forest

An accordion of lizard sweat
unfolding across our grandparents'
cloak of borrowed feathers
when a corpulent cloud
falls headless
from the dome
pulling down
the turquoise
embroidery some
among us
still yearn for
Dearest Mighty Little Fleabags
primal yappers of ironclad sentimentality
that encrusted virgin
chained to our foul mist
is this not a sign
that sagacity has
finally fled
our maddening slopes
abandoning us
to the dreams of salt's
uncharitable aspirations
Or is it pointedly odious
to advocate against
further unraveling
to prefer instead
the intractable cultivation
of our minor skills of admission
to the wooden shoes
operating on galvanic batteries
known as efficiency
when colossal ugliness
dominates earth's perpetual tilt
Might not our irritated interiors
abolish the indignities

we pay homage to
even as imagination's reptiles
import their tasteless banter
Are all our valves clogged shut
by sun's fixated grin
Is there no external partition
that adulterates our newest calamities
Imbecilic though they might be
this is the card machine's
plundered topography of grammar
we must submit to
lest we immerse ourselves
in the army of rankled vegetation
manufacturing
cabinet ministers
and the pittance
they bequeath us
in the name of hope
For as we are the sole
dictators of our own
minds and bodies
unsound in all
their stippled drops
can we not convince
the scenery to stop
thrashing us with
its inexcusable beauty
Are there no worthwhile
amendments to be advanced
our foreheads neatly dotted
with irregular tooth marks

IV.

In the Fourth Year of the Plague

Oil began dripping from the black and violet clouds bunched together near the top of the back stairs. In the second year of this calamity a caravan of hot-air balloons approached the bottled city. At least three of the pilots claimed to have witnessed a molten sky slide off heaven's domed ceiling. It was, they feared, further proof that they had drifted away from their appointed destinations, and had unwittingly entered a time of increasing vengeance and relentless cataclysm. Even the flowers fomented. And, as widely reported in a previously taped segment, this was an unheard-of metamorphosis that eventually drove the Royal Gardener and his cadre of young helpers to pronounce themselves insane and thus beyond all hope of repair.

How many disasters had been dutifully recorded in the ledgers before the beggars pitched forward in the streets? their corpses hauled away in the first hours of dawn. Every morning the sky thickened with smoke. By that time I was already a lonely child who talked to small creatures, and made detailed drawings of their pitchfork tongues, arched backs, and ribbed wings. My tongue grew black from licking the silver nibs, my fingers darkened like the river where the pails of ashes sank.

I was told that it was all an error in communication. A monumental slippage, it was announced, whose final outcome remains to be delivered to those who are fervent in their strict adherence to the old ways. Instructed not to ask more, I stopped talking altogether, and have continued to remain silent whenever I migrate through the spheres marked "Public" and "Off Limits."

My tutors and I passed the hours watching rain gather its bubble in the saltshakers our ancestors placed on the limestone altar behind the stables. I discovered that salamander is not a language you can learn in a reflecting pool. Their itinerary was neither heroic nor glittering, and they preferred to congregate in the muddy lanes encircling the arsenal. When you are made of invisible ink, I told my last bodyguard, you are pursued by vexations, but you are not yet the sordid creation you will one day inhabit, comfortable as fur wrapped in muslin and carried down from the mountains. I became the animals that appeared in my dreams, their longing remains my guide.

Listen, Little Magdalena Snowdrop, don't you think it's time we prepare another canvas?

All the World

The ant marathon has ended, but no one knows when the next round of insect rallies will start. The people in the front rows of the latest fashion are arguing about this and other less important matters, and those of us perched in the back rows, and there are far more of us than there are seats, can't tell which entrance in the hours erected by the sky's solid facade might prove useful should the mounting chatter take a turn for the worse, and the waters of our blooming roadkill begin backing up into the fountain that was once the pride of our town. The remaining elders want to migrate to the base of the canyon, but the audience's reactions prevent them from doing so. A woman in maroon taffeta sends Morse code to those living in the suburbs. A spider drops down from the rafters, a black pearl suspended in time and space.

The lead actor didn't live up to the advance billing, but few ever do, and those who exceed the audience's expectations are soon drowned out by the chorus, that collection of motley warthogs and pokey porcupines that magazine editors try to honor with medals of disputable merit. On the front is the engraving of a lost time, scenes of which flash like a sheriff's badge, with a regularity that introduces a higher level of comfort to those who crave it, like the men that set their watches according to the footsteps of the village idiot, who stops twice each day to yell at the mortal remains of our beloved mayor. Just as this scene was thankfully excised from the opera because the depths of bad taste plumbed by the librettist had finally reached a scandalous depth even his most faithful fans found beyond their tolerance.

As I was saying, the play was a great success during the early stages of its rehearsal, before the dialogs, monologs, asides, and unforeseen interruptions from the anarchist wing of the chorus began to be chiseled into the curtains that often represent clouds in certain respectable epics. After that, we visited the lovers who had taken up residence in an orange tollbooth. The path was steep and winding, and the audience gasped when we finally emerged on the rocky escarpment. An unexpected chill entered the scene, a sure signal that more was about to happen, perhaps in leaps and bounds. From then on, it was impossible to ignore our appointment with the sensitive fingers of the polygraph. We will never confess that we are mice. Never. It is not in our nature, whatever that is.

In the Now Lost Film

Paradiso Diaspora, after finding a sacred amphora, scared cadres desecrate the rim of its unrinsed interior. Reprise roles lost when the Nile started flowing into the Danube, and the Thames overflowed its banks. Is it true that the Aztec pyramids sank into a lake as still and turquoise as a photograph pinned beneath the sky's crumbling archways? Awhirl in rumors brought on by the flies in their gold hats and multiple eyes. Begin rummaging through silhouettes and escaped shadows.

A discredited surgeon removes the murkier parts and ships them to the Assistant Vice President of a mid-sized bank discreetly parked in a small town overlooking an unused section of the river. Muddy dinner plates are brought to the corner table. Beneath its black and gummy slab, a dog whimpers uncontrollably because its ventriloquist has lost his tongue.

The scene shifts to a hotel room occupied by a tall woman with freckles on her calves and a man of indeterminate height whose hair appears to be gray. In an unexpected combination of blazing speed and masterful penmanship, two black rabbits observing the scene pass detailed letters and diagrams back and forth. Years later, they reenact the intricacies they claim to have witnessed, and, often in the lean months of winter, elaborated upon around the fire, but this part gets lost when the couple meet after many years in a remote balcony, and begin exchanging corresponding wavelengths, after the wind dies down, and the plastic wolves howling along the ridge can no longer be heard by those who have inserted themselves into the pleats of the auditorium.

They have sworn not to swear allegiance to any country that claims to have been destined to exist. They live inside each other even when they are apart. They delete everything but their tears, which rise to the clouds. And since you ask, Cecil and Cecilia are neither their names nor their pseudonyms.

Downstream, a camera raises its incandescent black lids. A sleepy thirsty slitherer mounted on a titanium tripod. Surveys and calculates, before fondling the hors d'oeuvres of each repentant pulse ticking in the pants and dresses of the available. A velvet alligator interrupts this panoramic view to hug you. And it is you—the reader—who is sitting in the chair, waiting to see the satin doors part their moist threadbare lips. Receding rows of indigo light vanish beneath an artificial horizon bordered by imported flowers.

Even to those who remained steadfast in their sordidness, their neighbors' swift descent into decadence was bewildering.

After posing as small-time professors in love with a skittish fruit grower, three prematurely bald treasury agents decide they must murder the two-timing scriptwriter who plunked them on the gnawed benches of a dress factory owned and operated by a management platoon of sultry Amazons.

The tallest is hired by a Phoenix mobster to trace the outline of a woman he met at an abductor's support group, though he has no memory of how he got there. Here, things get fuzzy (or should I insert *fizzy*) and sky's doors are bolted shut against any further assaults.

The sun is a badge worn down by its responsibilities. You have only to look through the camera of your own eyes to see what you are talking about.

Postcard without Image

There are a few things you should know before we start kissing. Everything you heard about me is true, including the part about me dressing up as a deodorant and running through the supermarket aisles warning the shoppers of the doom that was about to befall them. It was just a phase, and a glorious one at that, full of so much promise, with the golden notes of the oncoming winter trembling in the cool autumn air. I was never the same after I fell out of the tree and landed in a passing truck. A few nicknames stuck, but none of them stayed long enough for me to remember where they came from, and how they got to my doorstep. I was born beside a dead battery that used to be connected to the skull grinning in the window of my uncle's wax museum. Sometimes I forget who I am and call the wrong number, but this can happen to anyone, particularly if they believe it is necessary to obtain items while they are on sale. I rented a table at a trade conference without bringing anything to trade. I sat outside Plato's Cave and waited for the shadows to emerge until I learned that I might be one too. I keep a few extras in the pond. My organs are similar to those you would find in a stuffed iguana. I didn't need to shave until it was bedtime, and all the elves had removed their hats before entering the beehive. The door you are looking for is just behind you. Yes, I have much more to tell you, but I will do that in due time. Meanwhile, is this your shoulder or mine?

Portrait with Still-Life

I find no reason to distract my father who is yelling at the empty prescription bottle. After he returned from the war, which he didn't find to his liking, he operated a drill press without distinction for nearly fifty years. He raised a family that was barely passable. He strode forth only when the weather fit his shoes. He stood in the backyard and painted all the landscapes that passed through his head, "like tulip petals on their way to a fatter version of heaven." He learned to read when he was a very young child, but found this was an impediment later in his life. He was not my father, but a kitchen appliance in need of repairs.

Don't Get Too Personal

Suppose you learned that I am a duck, a tall duck, but a duck nevertheless. Would you still keep your promise? Would you still meet me at the bowling alley on the edge of town, just beyond the circumference of streetlamps and radar towers that keep you in their sights? Or would you trade me in for a turkey, whose dumbness is legendary among amphibians, or call a condor, that dark fedora of the soul, to swoop in on the evening wind? Haven't we by now left the parking lot of nitpicking behind?

Here are a few of my finer points. I am a straight arrow that arrives in a clean car. No crumpled cups and cans gathering on the back seat. No substitute odors. Just an infusion of nature's sweet decay accompanied by soft music, the kind that you can rub your hands on and not get wet. There was a time when I didn't know what I know now. This was before other hands sketched in the parts I couldn't see.

Will it bother you that I waddle when I walk?

Look, I never claimed to be perfect. I am just saying that it's not out of my reach.

How I Pass My Days

Soft red feathers twirl down from a prematurely black sky. Shortly after
I receded from my nap I knew that I had been misled. That's what happens
when you consult a talking dog about what the future has crammed in its
warehouse. Not only doesn't it come with a lifetime guarantee, but it is
always more unreliable when it comes to sorting through rumors. For like all
canines with a predilection for making small talk, this one paraded forth all
the jokes it had stored in its semi-mechanized data bank, even the ones that
hadn't yet been repeated in the dimly lit parking lots that hem in every
hospital. I was still smarting from having been smitten in a ziggurat. The
bottoms of my feet itched, my eyes were watery. A snake danced in my
glass, but still I didn't suspect anything. And now I am strangely comforted
by the dog's increasingly outlandish lies, and the two well-manicured
vultures playing Hearts by the front door, waiting to see if any other
stragglers pop up on the radar screen.

Short Movie with Long Cartoons

Shortly after making an emergency landing on a loading dock stacked with cases of frozen fish, the oddly spotted puffin stopped huffing. Repeat and insert. The camera reverses itself, causing the two figures on the paisley covered cot to revisit their monuments to trembling. Toes unclench, hair turns back into coarse red turban. Tuscan sun rises over postcard.

From the row of windows floating above their shadows one can see the subway entrance, which has been hewn out of the side of a granite tower. Organized with asphalt and concrete, a non-descript hill descends to the river, passing the factory where they engage heating devices and ritual foot sponging. On the other side of the parking lot a bridge crammed with motorists.

We inhabit many lives to varying degrees, and some of them intersect, like the slender ribs of a Chinese fan held by the young girl in the painting. Languorous and drenched in her daily delirium, she will grow up and become someone I meet behind a pinstriped bowling alley, shortly before the pins are no longer able to withstand another assault on their fading sovereignty. In the interlude preceding the sun's debut at its appointed hour, we hold hands and eat oversized tulips, giddy with phrases like "subpoenaed moonlight," "moo goo gai pan in the rain" and "cement barge."

In the second chapter, we told each other stories about how we ended up on a gravel path circumnavigating a town known for the fires burning in its subterranean deposits. Throughout our long journey, we never succumbed to exchanging knickknacks or signing postcards of animals saying funny things. Later, we would read in the report that you are a rubber ant and I am a frog wearing sunglasses and matching hat, my skin vulnerable to being plucked by the sun. Black sand tumbles in the whirlpools.

I told you that I called the babysitter "Fire" when I stood up in my high chair and shit in the cereal bowl engraved with the family crest. You said confession wasn't necessary if we were going to begin fresh, which we had, first in a parking lot and then in a city known for its potbellied men and bowlegged women.

The children like to keep spiders in their biscuits.

It is why I never eat bread while playing the piano.

Get Together

Technically, aside from you might call a diminutive blemish, there is really nothing very wrong with me. I don't have to hide behind a rock during daylight hours, if you know what I mean. I am sure that, distasteful as they must have been, even a person of your mythic stature has had more than your share of unwanted encounters with those whom fortune found it necessary to frown upon. Okay, a few minor brushes with backstabbers of the law, but those gunnysacks are part of the gauntlet each dawn delivers. Besides, that ledger's locked in the bottom drawer of the irretrievable past, and we're on this bird-infested island, just you and me, two unattached pronouns waiting for long distance to kick in, so we can go down our respective paths to the launch pad. In the meantime, I know this is probably not the ideal time to conduct an interview, but I have a few questions I would like to ask, nothing personal you understand, but do you know what happened to the rest of your horoscope? I mean, can you tell me why all your telltale signs are missing?

Footfall

Those brackets of the year are pressing in again. Birds have started preparing their nests for the nearest recycling plant, and neighbors from across the lake are taking time off from their pyramid of daily tasks to arrange their vows in the shape of library cards, a custom that dates back to when the library was still a bowler hat at the crossroads of two alleyways, and a large basalt frog greeted every child with belches as big and round as wagon wheels.

Why is a vow a clock whose three hands never manage to catch up with each other, and point at the same number? a wooly mammoth lugging Lithuanian tulip bulbs over a foot bridge in a remote province. Mist tumbles down untainted mountains toward the valley, its redolent rills and musty dells, where a famous magician rose into the sky one morning, never to be seen again. His alpaca cloak is a keepsake displayed in a vitrine in the lobby of the former library.

The town got a lot of use out of that dusty transfiguration, but the new library is much less flexible, like a pair of shoes that can never be properly broken in, and end up in the hall closet, their shininess a further sign of misplaced optimism.

What is the purpose of all this accumulation, these monuments and archives thick with disagreeable details, is a question that remains on the tip of our tongues, something we have been meaning to ask but never get around to doing. The answers—and there must be more than one—are not to be found in either the new library or its venerable predecessor. Yes, there have been rumors and even reports, which is when a rumor becomes officially declassified, that some of the neighbors want to make addendums, alter, or even do away with vows completely, that they are considered an unnecessary burden on the taxpayer looking for legitimate loopholes amidst the backstabbing that plagues any civilized gathering.

Of course, trying to find a way out of here is not to be taken lightly. Our ancestors were preoccupied with entrances and exits, with how one might get up and leave the room, and not be missed or, in some cases, detested when they were gone. The history of their vileness and vacancy would take up volumes that our young librarians don't have time to unpack, recent events being far more urgent than tales of beheaded ogres trying to find their way to the butcher's table. But next to our history, which some commentators see as a collection of unlabeled bottles wrapped in blankets in the basement, it will seem like a hand-tooled, leather-bound tome waiting to be pulled from a shelf on a black winter night. Years hence, the gleam of the gilt edges will be remembered as the first of many troubling signs, but that realization must wait until the moment is right, and the vast table is set.

Don't you just love the tasseled rungs rising toward the shelf marked, *Heaven's Messy Plot*? Yes, you might have something there, something you would want to notify the auctioneer about, an ill-gotten possession that would enable you to possess and openly fondle, behave badly without fear of repercussions. I always wanted to own an adobe penthouse in that crooked tower, where foreign correspondents would bring their own supply of toilet paper, and steaming meats would be served on delicate wooden plates. "But," as my father told me just before the neighbors clipped out his tongue, "this is not your destiny." Later, they mounted it on the wall, like the jeweled wing of a bird. A few lit candles and recited poems they learned before they were children.

This is how I began my present sojourn, setting out while the libraries were still burning on the vast plains surrounding the artificial craters, plumes of aquamarine smoke dissipating in the cool westerly breezes, and the soot settling softly on the brim of my bowler hat.

Temple of the Sailboats

My friend who repairs elevators tells me that on the first of this month he saw four flying saucers hovering over his garage, but that he has not seen them since, and, for some reason that he now thinks is inconsequential, he can no longer remember why he forgot to tell me this before. Kneeling at the edge of a pond populated by squanderers, my friend asks in all seriousness, what becomes of these saucers in the winter when they cannot enter another country and must abide here or perish?

The scenery hasn't changed much since the author was told that many subscribers were calling in sick. The palms in front of the library periodically ignite, nearby clouds vibrate, and white dust collects under our fingernails and in our hair. Time can change its face, but the boxers remain dazed and may never recover. On the fourth day of our long overdue vacation, we stop and erect tents in the field behind the Metropolitan Opera House. We are a diversion, and the dogs and bees know it. They are becoming increasingly rapacious, full of chagrin and obligatory delight.

Wind Gauge

Horace is baking bricks in the backyard oven, his embroidered chef's hat crammed over his frayed ears. Since dawn, batches of smoke have been swirling in unruly supplication. No news from the crumbling arches to the south, but Horace and I have only recently negotiated a proper contract. We go to the demolition derby whenever we can borrow the neighbor's car. During the winter we pray for the health of Persephone, who carries Horace's *Collected Poems* to Hades at the first sign of winter. On the second Sunday of every month, we take the express bus to Midas and Muddy, small towns where candles tremble in the summer dusk, to look for remaindered copies of his earlier tomes. The only remaining problem we have yet to solve is the Curator of Earthquakes. Each morning, his assistant promises that he will return my call. I have been trying to warn him that Horace and I like our food to curl on their plates, and that the deer are lost in a snowstorm of flies. But he is the kind of host who did not greet us when we entered the museum's collection, a pair of rinsed statuary from a bitter and defeated age.

Impulsive Confession

What else would you like to know about me? I still have the oblong case
my father found me in, when, as he said later, in a rare moment of full
disclosure, "the owl dropped a rusty music box into my enemy's best hat."
Beside him stood my stalwart mother, who was seldom more than a fable
illustrating her ignorance about childhood. I was briefly an apprentice to the
local warlock, a stable boy for the Black Adder, and then, after much
internal combustion followed by unsavory bouts of enforced intimacy, I
began slowly climbing the corporate ladder to my present mesa of success.
My position requires that I stash a silver hammer in my samovar. In addition
to being properly scanned, scoured, and tagged, the servants' mouths have
been sewn shut so their spirits can't defecate in the hall closet or umbrella
stand. They move in dotted lines, like defaced antiques at an estate sale.

After the storms abated, both the cows and the elves decided it would be best
to move into a nearby castle that overlooks a streambed filled
with dead leaves. As dusk falls, as it is known to do once every hundred
years, the able-bodied bipeds board up the entrance and remove all exterior
signs and wrap them in burlap, while the quadrupeds man the parapets. I am
paid to extinguish the ancient wind machine, and shut off the stream
threading its way under the house. This is how I mastered the art of
chicanery and became a truth serum salesman.

It is the custom to help the queen's lady-in-waiting choose a husband who
bears no apparent resemblance to any of his predecessors, each of whom
sleeps in a sheltering tattoo. My dog has been known to bark at the pesky
morons gathering in the woods behind the shed, even those who feel the cold
hammering against their hearts.

Here, drink this; it will cool those organ
pipes you've been dragging around for years.

Debatable Cornucopia

My father told me that I was the byproduct of an unnatural union that he had not been privy to. Thus, we got off on the wrong foot, and it took many etched bottles to finally find a path that was mutually agreeable to the both of us. As we each possessed a streak of independence fueled by primitive lightning, this pact did not last long, perhaps the first hours of the worst winter to embrace the mountain's iron helmet and long dress. He borrowed a horse he had no intention of returning, while I walked into town and got a job driving a taxi. This propelled me to places I would not have otherwise known: *Istanbul Alley*, where champion bowlers gathered on Saturdays; *The Street of the Dead Chinaman Who Occasionally Comes Back to Life*; *Cinema of Ice*; *Cineplex of Lambs Led to Slaughter*; *Necropolis of Rubber Bathing Caps*. I wish I could have made these places up, as it would be another way to go there, which I do when I am not driving.

The shutters are drawn and I have returned to the indoor swimming pool where I can eat my lunch and dream of the tall woman in pink shoes. Driving is a way to take your mind off work, debt, and other details that press their misshapen noses against your windshield; and they have been known to howl curses of such length that one can barely get to the next stop sign without stopping for some cool refreshment, a negroni or mint julep. At the bar I meet a woman who invites me to her apartment on one condition, which she won't tell me until I accept her offer. I give her my last three lottery tickets and copy her phone number and address backward on my forehead, where it will be easy to read in the rearview mirror. Lately, the days seem intent on tightening their noose around the sun.

The remaining clouds peel off the granite wall rising behind the sky; with some drifting lazily toward the gutter where I have been standing for days, waiting for my hat to be delivered. What did you say your name used to be?

Concerto in C Minor

As the aluminum convertible's valves had been repeatedly misfiring the evening before, just after they had returned from the water cooler at the center of the earth, the freckled doll with big liquid eyes decided to transport her alligator twins in matching eggcups. All the others had already safely disembarked from their coaches. Their drivers smoked cigars and guffawed into their leathery hands, a private joke circulating among them, like a butterfly. Warm pink sunlight was filling the arched windows of the sitting room. The one-eyed violinist stopped to chew another wad of blue tobacco, while the rest of the chamber orchestra were busy tapping and plucking their makeshift instruments, including the lacquered ones that had been shipped from Shanghai shortly after I retired from my duties at sea.

And then I woke up and saw that all before me was as I had dreamed it would be. The young duchess, who was famous throughout Paris for the length of her thick red tresses, had finally arrived in her shiny, studded, black cabriolet, attended to by an endless stream of well-appointed mice, some of whom would run to and fro, making sure nothing untoward would occur on the streets ahead. The sight of distress and affliction was not unknown to her, as many people had mistakenly surmised, but the whispering was a problem that was not so easy to overturn. Only the mice, which had been genetically altered, were quick enough to nip it in the bud. Meanwhile, the duke was nowhere to be found, which is always how it should be when secret lovers meet in the morning, ready to commence with their rollicking.

You didn't write after that, but everything was fine in the tree house, where the gramophone was plugged into the sky, and the notes poured forth, punctuating the riverboat's whistle with a melancholy that caused the wolves to regret all the eggs they had hijacked from the royal chicken coop. I myself was unexplainably gladdened by the lugubrious tenor recounting the downward spiral of his love's last days, and never once stopped to consider it might be a reflection on my spent youth. It had stopped snowing, and the sight of three-legged deer prancing gracefully across the stage transfixed the audience's eyes.

The billboards lining the highway like lint were getting increasingly vituperative, with the ones closest to the capitol making claims no one dared dispute, lest their hair fall out in clumps and their eyes begin boiling in their sockets. That would not be a pretty sight, whispered my aunt Velma with a glee she usually reserved for her weekend gin and mahjong marathons. Lately I had started to notice that she was getting tipsier earlier in the week, and that soon the end of one binge and the beginning of another would overlap, leaving her little time to run the computer repair shop that she had inherited from her late husband, Zack.

Of course, the dream wasn't really a dream, but a portent of things to come, the changing of the seasons, the subtractions that would never be replaced, and the ledgers that the punctilious squirrels kept year after year, issuing massive decrees even when the plague threatened to throttle the economic upswing initiated by the small industries that had moved out of the cottages and farms, and relocated their operations in the empty laboratories dotting the landscape with their defunct warning signs. Some of the newer inmates have started praising the signs, but, alas, I am not one of them.

Fourteen Future Tales

What association can any one of us belong to without squaring the remains of the tattered sky? I am a newly elected bridesmaid of the Missing Companion Society. In addition to being a retired tourist and a collector of counterfeit folklore, I am a gold-flecked introduction to the untrammeled lots of retail empires stretching east. When I was young I enjoyed dancing, but I did not enjoy making people dance. I am a specialist in last snapshots, the one who pours directly into the glass. I am a backward glance of the qualitative changes that took place near the end of the era of mass production. I used to live in Egypt before it turned its façade of falcons toward the Mediterranean, its churning mudflats.

In the middle of a parking lot bright with colored tiles from Bayonne and Ravenna is a magnificent aluminum fountain. A stained octagonal sign asks visitors to speak in an audible whisper. Two dirt roads embrace the ticket stand, where nature is no longer a hieroglyphic text in need of study. And beside the ditch of holy water, as the afternoon begins slipping off its propaganda shelf, a phalanx of pheasants dutifully trudges among its feathered replicas.

On the eve of our most solemn and blessed occasion, we gather in the pantry and draw straws, but none of them fit.

Final Notice

The President of the Moth and Blanket Society formally announces that he will no longer be requiring your services, and that it is better if, from now on, your whereabouts are a mystery to all those who might wish to inquire after you. You might remember that the druggist sent his youngest daughter a mask of an ex-dictator who recently was hired as an official greeter at a Las Vegas nightclub. After she shaved its head, she carefully swept the hair into a glassine envelope and sent it to her lover, a grammarian known for his research of weather patterns infiltrating the enemy lines. In the week before Halloween, when the decision was made, pranksters began papering over the moon's billboard with emerald snowflakes and posters that smelled of rotten pineapples. The oldest boys were determined to reach the top of the ladder, where a gargoyle munched on hot dogs slathered with motor oil. The mountain climbers greeted his hideous vocabulary with porcupine indifference. The vase is permitted a solitude that is denied the rose and rattlesnake. I tap the investment portfolio with a chopstick.

She stood by the door. Cleaning the X proved hazardous to the others who had preceded her. The monkeys fled the garden. In the case of lime and orange, she liked the colors but not the fruit. A sponge soaked up the ink, leaving the steamer stranded by some previously invisible rocks. The captain pointed to the funicular.

He is said to be the first who froze his semen. It is a kind of poetry, he exclaimed, though he did not go so far as to say what kind.

Last Confession

This is what I told you after we first undressed. I always thought that one of my chief skills was not to occupy myself with questions that do not concern me. For example, my cat Titian has always been fond of academic nudes, especially after a rainstorm when pockets of moisture hover above the down circling their sooty wrists.

The Umbrella School can be divided into roughly two periods, before the grotesque reached its zenith, and after the alphabet was lost in a crooked card game.

There are many unimportant influences that have yet to be applied to the overall scheme, most pointedly in small towns where the production of color introduces a distasteful aroma to the surrounding countryside, and all the adolescent rabbits move away.

You said: Yes, it is food for thought to leave one's life behind, particularly if that one is overrun by angry mice, and the angriest of all the mice demands you address him in the proper manner.

So began our life as stowaways on a ship that is drifting closer to the sun.

V

The Morning after That One

The telling will go on for many years until the last one that was there expires. There is here. Here is the gridded set of coordinates by which you will tell where in the there you learned that time had been slowed down, stretched out, turned over, and repeated. The story begins with the coordinates, with the measures and markers one used to deduce one's movements toward and away. Unable to stop, to come to a point of rest, one became the mind and body of a gyroscope, became a mouth speaking.

How many orbits did any one of us find ourselves in? This is the gravitational pull of that day's persistent questions. Where in relation to what? Where in relation to where? Could one account for all one's pronouns?

The telling of the story begins with the intersection of geography and time, where and when. Of this story there are many tellings. This one begins before the 6:20 A.M. Silver Meteor departs for Miami, stopping at Baltimore. The hours between departing and stopping are when he sleeps.

Somewhere past Wilmington he wakes up and sees little puffs of fog hugging the still wet grass. And this one begins around 10:00 A.M., on a subway to Penn Station. A description of the woman who helps you lift the baby carriage onto the platform.

These stories meet in a present whose boundaries keep moving past the horizon, as you and I become silhouettes sitting in someone else's house, watching the story begin again and again. Impossible to leave this room which is inside a room whose air is burning. Beneath sky's black roof time both starts and stops, spirals back on itself, becomes a wheel spinning back to the first moments of that day, coffee's heated molecules dispersing into the air, garbage truck engine idling as its hydraulic gears lift a sheet metal container briefly skyward. Sky still dark, streets still empty.

How close or far is the answer that asks to be told. The question is unspoken, need not be asked, is in the air between. One hesitates to ask more, knowing more will come. Of when and where one first saw or learned what others were seeing. Of these minutes. One has to see them passing. One has to see them again. One does not ask how long it will take to remember what one has watched again and again.

For months afterward she would talk about the sculptor who said the events of that day would not affect his work. Her story includes his story, but she realizes that his story does not include hers. She can neither accept nor understand this.

I place these smaller stories, these shards, in front of the larger one and ones. I do not offer them as offerings.

Eleven Months Is Not a Year
(for Kippy Stroud)

On my way to the post office to mail photographs of my daughter—she is sixteen months old—to a friend living in Lawrence, Kansas (I haven't seen her in six or seven years), I hear someone behind me talking in a loud voice: "Someone said you killed her before you loved her. Someone said you did it and you don't know if you did or not. You didn't love someone you didn't know. You don't know if you did it."

I turn and see that he is talking to himself rather than talking on a cell phone and I am relieved, if only for a moment.

Yesterday, in the paper, I read that a street vendor had been found in a hospital, suffering from amnesia. He had been missing since the morning of September 11, 2001, nearly eleven months ago. He remembers neither what happened nor who he is. And until a few weeks ago, no one in the hospital had been able to figure out who might know him.

This summer, while my family and I were staying on Mount Desert Island, Maine, we drove around the sparsely inhabited island a number of times. Often it was because we were lost. On one road, which connected two small towns at the far end of the island, the side closest to the ocean and furthest from the mainland, we passed a small, run-down ranch house. It was one of a handful of houses on a stretch of the road few people would pass, even in the summer months. Bar Harbor is the primary destination for those who visit Mount Desert Island in the summer, and this road is about as far as you can be from Bar Harbor and still be on the island.

A painted wooden sculpture was erected in the middle of the overgrown lawn; it was silhouettes of firemen in yellow raincoats hoisting the American flag. They are posed exactly as in the *Life* magazine photograph of American soldiers hoisting the flag on Iwo Jima. Supposedly, this flag raising is an impromptu ceremony that occurred at the end of a long and decisive battle.

The collapsing together of two events, one that took place in the Pacific during World War II and the other that occurred in New York less than a year ago, is a sign of our confusion, our inability to understand what happened, has happened, is happening. We have to see it through the lens of another event, one that in this case happened more than half a century ago. And that event was staged, which haunted one of the men in the photograph.

The *Life* photograph was evidence that the Americans had won a crucial victory; they had gained control of the island of Iwo Jima in their march toward Japan. By echoing this staged photograph, the people living in the ranch house are expressing the desire that Americans regain control of another island, Manhattan.

The man walking behind me was talking about himself in the second person, he had lost his "I." He and the amnesiac had this loss in common. The family living in Maine uses a "we" that first appeared in a staged photograph, a theatricalized moment. Years later, in the late 1950s I believe, there was a B film of one of the soldiers, an early version of what we would now call a biopic. The soldier was a Native American.

I remember a scene of a man drinking beneath a pulsing night sky. He thought of himself as a sham rather than as a hero and began drinking shortly after his neighbors welcomed him home. Soon afterward he died, distraught from all the notoriety the photograph had conferred upon him.

This morning, before I began writing, I wondered if I was confusing two different stories, but I am not even sure what two I would be confusing.

A few minutes ago, my friend Jeremy called and apologized for not calling yesterday, when he said he would. When I asked him why, he said, "I totally spaced it. I was just sitting in the apartment staring at nothing."

I tell him in the last week that I have lost my ATM card, and a computer disc given to me by a poet and friend; it contained his translations, and something else, though I can't remember now what it was.

We talk about the weather, how it is cooling down, the same as it did a year ago. I tell Jeremy I can't remember where I left my ATM card, but I know that I lost the computer disc somewhere between Kinko's and where I live, somewhere on Fifth Avenue near the Empire State Building which I pass whenever I go to have something copied.

During the past few weeks, whenever I am walking on Fifth Avenue near the Empire State Building, I stop and look at the people taking photographs of their friends posing with the building rising in the background. I wonder how much of the building will appear in their photographs.

The man talking to himself doesn't know if he did something heinous or not. The man in the hospital doesn't remember what happened to him. The family on Mount Desert Island tries to understand what they saw over and over on television. None of them have found refuge. In that, and perhaps only that, they are not alone.

Sotto Voce

It is raining in New York. Raining and raining.
The sky is full of confetti, but it is not confetti.
In a letter dated April 3, 1870, Mallarme wrote:
"I don't know which of my internal climates
I should explore in order to find you and meet you."
The aurochs and orangutans are restless.
Far-flung crinoline stump patter.
For a week now, not a single cockroach has been spotted.
Conform confound confront congratulate.
I am not perturbed by your pertinacity.
In the clerestory Cleopatra clenches a clerk.
The spider moves to the ceiling.
She was born in a forty room house in Shanghai
and died in a six room house in Burlington, Mass., not far from the mall.
Monks are not allowed to talk at meals, nor think of food.
John Wilkes Booth was the son of Junius Brutus Booth.
There is a statue of John's brother, Edwin, in Gramercy Park.
Let us consider some theories explaining reincarnation via hypnosis.
In August 1914, as the world was crumbling, Kandinsky
traveled from Munich to Switzerland to Russia.
An out-of-the-body experience may have its roots in childhood trauma.
The Moroccan cab driver tells me that it is no longer possible to leave
Manhattan, all the bridges are closed until further notice,
and the subways are finally undergoing repair.
Is it important that my socks don't match?
On a day when a famous magician is unable
to return from the place he sent himself,
a small errand he told the audience.
I Will Only Be a Minute becomes a headline
that a man in a bright blue suit with oversized lapels
would rather forget, as he quaffs more coffee
from a flawless pink porcelain cup
he found in a flea market run by Russian émigrés.
I have eaten ostrich, muskrat, and small pets.
When he was sixteen, his mother asked him to move out

as she thought his room would be put to better use if a servant slept in it.
"The I," Wittgenstein wrote, "is not an object.
I objectively confront every object. But not the I."
Years after he walked through grizzly bear country
alone, and shortly after he told his hostess
it had been a "wonderful evening,"
he put a gun to his head and pulled the trigger.
The empress of Fiji once asked me for directions
to a hotel known for its international clientele
but I didn't know that Fiji has no empress.
The fountain is gray only when the temperature goes below freezing.
The parrot next door has started speaking Spanish.
The toy repair man wants to name his children
after the capitals of states that end in "a".
I always keep twelve cans of meatballs in the front closet.
The kangaroo is tired of practicing for his upcoming match.
A stack of postcards from the Bonn train station.
I was sent because I had a clean slate and was well versed
in the art of handling a fork and a steam shovel.
It is quite possible that Manchuria
in the initial postglacial period
was covered by woods.
The last time we spoke he told me he had five jobs:
luggage handler, supermarket shelver, part owner of a baseball
memorabilia store, taxi driver, and clerk.
Hart Crane jumped off the bow of the Orizaba.
The vampire unbuckled his shoes and stretched out
on a pile of newspapers that have been delivered to the wrong address.
My uncle was a plumber who had no knack for the job.
On a shelf in the bedroom are seventeen mice that run on batteries.
If in your dream you encounter a dunghill,
money will arrive through the most unexpected sources.
On the landing in the back hall I see that I live on
the thirty-third floor of an eight story building.
My parents lie side by side in an unmarked grave
at the bottom of a hill in a suburban cemetery
surrounded by a chain-link fence.
I have had many nicknames and liked none of them.

A passion for idealized reality and attractive surfaces,
rendered with excessive, almost fanatical precision,
are common features of the period. All morning,
countless throngs of hard and sparkling elements
with rounded contours descend and dissolve.
Stamps from Italy and Borneo.
The emperor has dispatched the orchestra director on a fast horse
to find Li Po, who is sprawled across a table in a local wine shop.
Outside, the dogs have started barking,
though no one predicted this would happen.
I am nearly fifty-three, my daughter is not yet two.
Samuel Rosenstock is better known as Tristan Tzara.
At the age of forty he had a revelation and decided
that he should be president. An instrument
that measures electrical potentials on the scalp
and generates a record of the brain's electrical activity.
Is it a mere accident that the jawbone of a skeleton was chosen to represent
such an important mathematical symbol?
Talon, talus, tamale, tamarack, tamarind.
One of Guirdjieff's most devoted students
was Olga Ivanovna Hinzenburg,
who was married to Frank Lloyd Wright.
The Russians, it has been claimed, are using a giant
Tesla magnifying transmitter to modify the world's weather,
creating extremes of ice and drought.
In 1935, the *New York American* blasted
the famous explorer F.A. Mitchell-Hedges,
because he had written: "Atlantis existed.
Its engulfment caused 'The Flood,'
a cataclysm that wiped out millions."
Hidden valleys that shelter a hard existence
for a precious few, bald sun-scorched mountains,
nearly impracticable roads washed out
half the time by raging torrents, and yet
a fascinating wild beauty bathed in extraordinary light.
Photographs show Madame Blavatsky to have possessed
strong arms, several chins, and slightly bulging eyes.
In Zagora, the last stop before "gazelle country,"

there is a hotel with a swimming pool.
Bacteriologically pure and therefore theoretically fit to drink.
At the end of August, we flew from Rome to London
to see Leonardo's "Deluge" drawings.
Romanus realized that the hunt for heretics
had to be intensified, but he was not very successful
in devising new methods to find them.
The sky is full, but it is not.
Then the devil went to the gate of paradise,
wanting to enter, and could not.
He remained at the gate a thousand years.
Plumes of the white egret were used to make
ceremonial wands and military insignias.
He claimed to have been wounded in Tibet in 1902,
while on a mission there to study occult lore.
The painting made the first leg of its journey
from Venice to Baghdad by boat,
wrapped in velvet and waterproof canvas,
its existence incontrovertible proof
that likeness could be attained.
The true vegetable elixir has a pseudo-alchemical name:
"returned cinnabar with a wrinkled face."
I never washed my coat and rarely took it off.
In a matter of hours maybe days perhaps weeks
but certainly not years it will rise above my windows.

VI

In the Garden of Books
(after Eugenio de Andrade)

Que fizeste dar palavras
What did you do with the words

and their shadows
impregnating books

you slowly opened
and swiftly closed

carried across time zones
and temperate zones

zones of influence
and conflict

And what did you do
with the shadows

stuck between pages
the ones that ran

and the ones that fell
and the ones that dissolved

on the sinuous paths
of lawn and of moss

What explanation of their consonants
did you use for crimes of the heart

and the statue missing
its other head

Did they also tell
of aqueducts and astrolabes

the magic stone
a child forgets in the grass

What relation to the vowels
did you sing of

before birds
rose into the sky

Did they speak of
burning doorways

fearsome laughter
and creeping about

of being lost among
the dying bowers

and hemlock flowers

In the Kingdom of Poetry
(after Carlos Drummond de Andrade)

Don't write poems
about yourself.

Don't call attention
to your revelations

or make confessions.
Even if your intention

is to expiate pain,
overcome guilt,

temper your
understandable anger,

don't excavate
your mother's grief,

brother's sexual torment,
sister's thievery,

father's self-hatred,
step-parent's fortuitous star chart.

Feelings are not poems.
Relatives should be left

where they are found,
in the gutter

or by a cash register.
Don't write poems

about others.
Leave out husbands,

divorcees, alcoholics,
pimply adolescents, and nurses.

There is already a surplus
of bad movie scripts.

Forget about friends
and enemies,

anniversaries
and special moments.

Someone in the greeting card business
has already covered these topics.

Don't write about
what is happening in the world,

the missing child
and the human remains,

the burning beach
and the swallowed page,

the president's
fiftieth speech.

Whatever happened there
isn't a poem.

Don't try and prove
how sensitive you are.

Others have already
claimed to be plants.

It isn't necessary to demonstrate
how insensitive you are

as this is already
an indisputable fact.

Don't write poems
linking

an ordinary event
in your life

—shaving, adjusting your bra, riding subway,
admiring especially picturesque sunset—

to a significant moment in history
—pogrom, starvation, exile, assassination—

or to a myth—rape, jealousy, or rejection—
in fact to anything that has a theme.

Poems are not papers
delivered at conferences.

Don't sing about the joys of the city
or list the virtues of rural life.

Don't mention swans,
bologna, eyeball dryness,

or one-eared philosophers.
Picnics and paintings are not poems.

Don't resort to drama
or telling lies.

Don't use your yearning
as a starting point.

Secrets should be left
where they are.

Don't stand up
in a burning theater

and announce,
"no one listens to poetry."

Don't write poems
about poets

being underpaid.
Throw away

your memories,
bury your mirrors.

John Yau is the author of over thirty books of poetry, fiction, and criticism, including *Ing Grish*, *Borrowed Love Poems*, *Hawaiian Cowboys*, and *The United States of Jasper Johns*. He edited an anthology of fiction, *Fetish*, organized a retrospective of Ed Moses's paintings and drawings for the Museum of Contemporary Art in Los Angeles, and contributed a long essay to the catalogue *In Company: Robert Creeley's Collaborations*. He has taught at Brown University; the University of California, Berkeley; the Milton Avery Graduate School of the Arts at Bard College; and the Maryland Institute College of Art. Since 2004, he has been an assistant professor of critical studies at Mason Gross School of the Arts at Rutgers. He has received awards and fellowships from the National Endowment for the Arts, the New York Foundation for the Arts, the Ingram Merrill Foundation, the GE Foundation, the Peter S. Reed Foundation, the Foundation for Contemporary Performance Art, and the Academy for American Poets. In 2006, he received a fellowship in poetry from the Guggenheim Foundation. He is the art editor for the *The Brooklyn Rail*, and his essays on contemporary art appear regularly in *Modern Painters*. He lives with his wife and daughter in Manhattan.